Terrific Tips for Parents

PAUL LEWIS

POCKET GUIDES

Tyndale House Publishers, Inc.

Wheaton, Illinois

Adapted from *Forty Ways to Teach Your Child Values,* copyright
1985 by Paul Lewis, Tyndale House Publishers, Inc.

Library of Congress Catalog Card Number 88-50089
ISBN 0-8423-7010-2
Copyright 1988 by Paul Lewis
Printed in the United States of America

CONTENTS

How to Use This Book

You're not holding an ordinary book on parenting. Actually, it's a handbook—a kind of super-condensed, quick reference guide to fifteen of the most important skills, attitudes, and values your toddler, junior, or teenager will need to grow into a mature and successful adult.

Each chapter outlines the basic principles and practices that you as a parent should observe in order to instill successfully in your child an important life skill or understanding.

Here's the best way to use this book.

First, look through the contents and pick a few of the skills, attitudes, or values your child is now dealing with or soon will be, or about which you as a parent are curious. Then read those chapters.

Second, read with a pencil in hand. You may want to mark many of the practical suggestions or activities you want to use. Some of the ideas will work best in one kind of parent-child relationship. Others will be best suited to a different mix of parent-child temperaments. Be sensitive to what feels most natural.

Finally, the appendix of this book, "Keeping Track," offers a helpful way to chart your child's growth—the areas that still need development and those that have become pretty well mastered. Write your child's name at the top of the checklist of the skills, attitudes, and values this book covers. Then use the rating system provided to evaluate his or her growth. If you have more than one child, additional checklists have been provided.

Now before you dive in, please consider these six truths effective parents must regularly review:

1. Children ultimately make their own choices.
2. If you think you've largely failed so far, it is never too late to start doing what's right.
3. Modeling is the bottom line.
4. No parent is an island.
5. A good marriage is more important in raising your child than excellent parenting skills.
6. Kids forgive and forget much easier and longer than parents do.

One of the wonderful ironies of parenting is that we can't know how well we've succeeded in our assignment until it's too late. And just when our on-the-job training is complete, we're unemployed. All the more reason to pay attention, keep a good sense of humor, and give our children the best model to learn from that we can. The rewards are more than worth it.

CHAPTER 1

The Enormous Gift of Self-Esteem

We see and hear the term *self-esteem* frequently. Troublesome behavior in children, even neurotic behavior in adults, we're told, stems from a lack of self-esteem. But what exactly is it? What does self-esteem accomplish? And where do these feelings originate, especially in children?

Put simply, feelings of self-worth are internal thoughts and beliefs. They tell you that you're a worthwhile person, and that you're reasonably competent and likeable. When you choose to believe these ideas about yourself, you then expect others to see you this way and to respond accordingly.

The chart below shows a cause-and-effect relationship between feelings and behavior.

SELF-ESTEEM

+ Self-concept	– Self-concept
worthwhile	unworthy
competent	incompetent
likeable	unlikeable

Behavior	Behavior
open	closed
friendly	hostile
optimistic	pessimistic
industrious	lazy or erratic

well-groomed	unconcerned or
	   hyperconcerned
	   about appearance

venturesome	constricted

When you understand this cause-and-effect relationship, it's not hard to see how your responses to your child become his or her primary source of self-esteem. And self-esteem is fundamentally established through the experiences of childhood. The patterns of thought begun there are very difficult to change later on.

DOs

Here, then, are some of the kinds of parental responses that will build healthy and positive feelings of self-esteem in your child. How do these compare with your present approach?

- First, take stock of your own reservoir of self-esteem. Parents need a positive self-image themselves in order to build one in their children.
- Provide a young child with opportunities to develop competence and confidence. Invest in toys, games, and crafts that enable the child to create and to succeed in mastering self and his or her environment.
- Allow your child to choose his or her own areas for achievement. Don't try to impose on your child the ambitions you had as a young person, or make him or her achieve what you didn't in sports, academics, or the arts.
- Genuinely listen to your child. It teaches the individual that he or she is an interesting person.
- Ask for your child's opinion about what to do in various problem situations. This will help the child discover that his or her judgment can be sound.
- If you raise questions (without ridicule) about your child's plans, you'll help the child find that he or she can be flexible and can reevaluate situations when new information is presented.
- See each child as an individual. Avoid comparing your children to each other. Emphasize unique strengths and weaknesses.
- Discuss your child—especially his or her problems—only when the child is not present.
- Be aware of your child's nicknames, especially those you use. Refrain from calling him

or her by derogatory names, or even seemingly innocent labels such as "Turtle" that might suggest undesirable qualities. Develop positive names such as "Champ" or "Little Lady."

- When a child is kind, unselfish, neat, helpful, self-disciplined, creative, well-coordinated, industrious, or anything else that's praiseworthy, say so! Your child will learn that he or she can be successful in these ways. Sincere praise never hurt anyone!
- Point out and applaud your child's improvements, no matter how small. He or she will learn to be optimistic.

DON'Ts
The opposite approach will obviously destroy self-esteem. Giving in to the tendency to be negative and condemning is the most effective way to make a child lose any sense of worth.

- Avoid condemning criticism and ridicule. They teach a child that something is basically wrong with him or her.
- Avoid constantly making decisions for your child. If you do, the child will conclude that his or her judgment is poor.
- Avoid pointing out your child's many failures and imperfections. It can only cause the child to lose any confidence in being competent. Soon the child will cease to like him or herself, and won't expect to be liked by anyone else, either. After all, "Dad and Mom are bigger, stronger, and smarter than I am, so

their judgment must be right. There's something wrong with me!"

Now reread the two sections above, noting which approaches describe your behavior toward your children. Based on this self-evaluation, what is your child concluding about him or herself?

What your child decides is terribly important. And only you can give the enormous gift of true self-esteem.

Three Building Blocks of Self-Esteem

1. The security of belonging. This comes from experiencing a solid position of significance in the family.
2. The satisfaction of achievement. Each child needs a chance to be successful at something—hopefully, many things.
3. The joy of feeling valued. A child's happy awareness that he or she is valuable is maintained through consistent, sincere praise.

Making and Keeping Friends

Among the essential skills of living, few are more crucial than understanding how to build and preserve good friendships. But what characterizes the art of making and being a friend? And how will your child learn it?

Both sociological research and common sense suggest that it begins largely with what you model as parents — the qualities of friendship your child observes in how you and your spouse treat and respond to each other. How do you handle your conflicts and express your joys? Does your child sense that you are not only spouses but also best friends?

But modeling isn't the only way you can teach your child about friendship. Let's learn some other ways.

THE ART OF BEING A FRIEND

1. *Preschool and kindergarten.* Your child's first six years are spent moving toward a sense of healthy separation from his or her parents, especially Mom. Friends are seen merely as

parallel travelers, which explains the child's frequent disregard for the interests of others. Self-centeredness must gradually give way to concern for others.

Play is the primary context at this age for learning good friendship skills. Take your three- or-four-year-old on an outing with two or three friends, for example. Notice his or her verbal and physical expressions of selfishness. Then, in a gentle, positive way, offer some ideas for alternative behavior.

2. *Elementary age.* As your child's comfortableness with autonomy grows, so will his or her attachment to others. During this stage, talk together frequently about his or her friends. Make up adventure stories and draw pictures that include these friends. Begin now to talk about the negative results of choosing poor friends.

Playing cooperative games helps build essential skills. Invite friends along on family outings and over for dinner. Take your child shopping for friends' birthday gifts, or help him or her make a simple toy, game, or craft as a gift. While you shop or work, talk about the feelings of affection you feel for various people you know, both within and outside your family.

3. *Preadolescence.* Gradually, your child's focus on relationships will move more to peers of the same sex and to adults outside the family. This "gang" helps him or her learn feelings of belonging and the confidence of having something valuable to offer. Scouting and other children's organizations are also healthy expressions of the desire to belong to a group.

Outings, slumber parties, overnight visits with friends, and short vacations with another family or group can be great fun. Your child's ability to stand alone when necessary in adolescence will be built on a foundation of being liked by friends. Understanding the kind of friends that should be chosen must be a continuing goal.

You may need at times to help your child evaluate and curb those friendships that are having a negative influence. And you'll likely need to help your child learn to appreciate and include in his or her circle of friends someone he or she doesn't see as likeable.

Throughout these preteen years, you are your child's sanctuary from those who reject his or her friendship. You also continue to be his or her model for reaching out to others.

How to Be a Good Friend

- Listen
- Be interested in others
- Seek others out
- Appreciate others
- Praise the good qualities of your friends
- Share genuine feelings
- Keep confidences

---

4. *Adolescence.* At this stage, children are moving through a self-reevaluation process, initially through group participation and acceptance, and later through more individual and

independent actions. During this time, you will have opportunities to express unconditional acceptance of your child and to model adult qualities of true friendship.

Take time to explore your feelings and those of your child. Discuss and list the qualities you look for in a friend. Talk also about the unpleasant side of friendship, such as jealousy, deciding between two friends, apologizing, and the death of a friendship.

If at this point you and your child aren't true friends, take steps to restore the relationship. This must begin with a genuine humbling, forgiveness, and reconciliation. These are the tough moments of friendship when wrong must be admitted and the truth spoken in love.

Your child's skill at initiating and nourishing good friendships will depend in large measure on the modeling and learning experiences you provide. It is especially critical for fathers to model friendship skills to sons as well as daughters. It's a great responsibility, but the happy fruit is a lifelong treasure of knowing your child as a genuine friend.

Creating Close Family Feelings

Underlying many of the important values you want your child to absorb is one so basic it often escapes notice. Yet in our rootless, transient culture, this critical value is undergoing extensive erosion. It's the value of family—that incredible laboratory where life makes up its mind.

Dr. Harold M. Voth, senior psychiatrist and psychoanalyst at the Menninger Foundation, observes, "The most serious crisis facing us today is that of the family, the alterations of its internal structure, the high incidence of its dissolution, and the associated crisis of the human spirit."

When your child leaves home, will it be with an unshakable commitment to fidelity in marriage and to the nuclear family model? The answer will be fashioned directly by your leadership in the family of which he or she is now a part. And three important principles will need to be part of his or her convictions about the family:

- The concept of family is fundamental to God's design for humanity. When the family is artificially altered, both society and individuals suffer and fall prey to a host of psychological ills and sociological diseases.

- The family unit is the foundation of individual security, identity, and connectedness. It's the best vehicle through which values and a sense of purpose and destiny can be transmitted. Without a sense of heritage and worth originating in the family, a profound crisis in personal identity is inevitable. No other institution can adequately replace the family. As historian Will Durant has observed, "The family can exist without the state, but without the family all is lost."

- Modeling is the primary way values and personal identity are transmitted in the family. If one grows up outside a traditional family unit, it is almost always more difficult to establish a successful family in the next generation.

TEN STEPS TO A POSITIVE FAMILY HERITAGE

Here are some ways to enhance the heritage and commitments your child will gain from life in your family.

- Talk about the distinctives and values to which your family is committed. Stress them through your conduct. Perhaps you could symbolize them in a family crest, displayed in a prominent spot. As these values are challenged from outside the family, rally together in mutual support.

- Stress family unity through activities and enjoyable hobbies in which every family member can participate. Build family traditions around these. Make matching family T-shirts or buttons that symbolize your unity and spirit.
- Take lots of pictures of your family in action together. Bring them out frequently for review. Make a family scrapbook of non-photo items that will also help you reminisce about family outings, achievements, and crises faced together. Frequently recite and praise the accomplishments and growth of family members as you review the albums and scrapbook together.
- Do some joint research into your family history. Use the genealogical section of your local library and talk with older relatives. Create a family tree and collect old family photos and artifacts.
- Write together a contemporary, ongoing history of your own family. You might begin with your marriage and include memorable family occasions up to the present. Write a biographical sketch of each family member that reflects his or her special traits, skills, and talents.
- Try to find out the meaning of your family name, as well as the meaning of each member's first and middle name. Books with such information are usually available at the local library.
- Make a habit of recording in a special notebook the funny, profound, or otherwise memorable sayings of each child.

- Keep in touch with relatives on both sides of your family. Include visits with them at holiday and vacation times. Keep a round-robin family newsletter circulating, and when it comes, gather the family to read it and enjoy the enclosed snapshots. Make a wall display or bulletin board of old family photos including as many relatives as possible.
- Periodically stage a family reunion. Emphasize accepting all family members just as they are, including the "black sheep," if any. Fill the time with talent shows, skits that relive episodes in the lives of family members and ancestors, and prizes for the oldest, youngest, worst dressed, tallest, or anything else you can think of. Plan plenty of time for older family members to speak of their past. Take a group photograph and work on charting a family tree. Have everyone bring old photos and family artifacts to share.

  Note: If your family has been broken by death or divorce, work at keeping alive every positive connection and look for other individuals, couples, or families with which a surrogate family bond can be built. If grandparents live far away, allow your kids to adopt older friends who live nearby as another set of grandparents.
- As much as possible, resist our society's tendency to separate people into age groups. This practice erodes the interaction needed to pass along traditional values and cultural continuity across generations. Our moral and cultural chaos today is probably at least in part a reflection of this profound loss.

CHAPTER
4

What Is Your Child Learning about Sex?

Human sexuality is one of the most exploited and bankrupt aspects of our culture. Helping your children gain and practice a balanced and biblical view of sexuality is a difficult assignment, but you as a parent are in the best position to teach them about sex. You provide a positive context of warmth, love, and security in which healthy attitudes toward sexuality can be cultivated.

Unfortunately, too many parents leave this critical part of their child's development to teachers or peers. In a survey of teenagers some years ago, only one in fourteen kids had received sex information from their parents before they had heard about it from friends! With teenage sexual experimentation and pregnancy rates still growing, compounded by the danger of AIDS, the need for developing a wholesome, God-honoring attitude toward sex is more important than ever.

A person's attitudes about sex are always tied to his level of emotional maturity and sense of self-esteem. So, use some basic developmental principles to match a child's readiness to learn with strategies for learning.

KEY TEACHING PRINCIPLES

- Your youngster's response to sexual urges will rise out of his experiences with life and love in general. By providing a positive and supportive emotional climate in your home, you convey that psychological intimacy and personal involvement are not to be feared— essential ingredients for developing a healthy attitude about sex.
- The attitudes your child has toward his or her body will color the child's view of sex. From your comments, "looks," and responses to your child's questions and self-explorations, he or she will develop feelings largely the same as the ones you have about your own body. This is an area of crucial concern in the earliest years.
- Friendly feelings between your child and the parent of the opposite sex will substantially condition his or her enjoyment of the other sex, as well as future sexual adjustments. The pleasure and open affection you and your spouse display toward each other is also essential modeling.
- Handling discipline in your home in a democratic way is important for positive sex education. The mutual respect, involvement, and commitment family democracy stresses will become a part of your child's sexual values, too.

TOWARD A HEALTHY VIEW
OF SEXUALITY

Here are some practical ways to give your child a healthy view of sexuality:

1. *Preschool and elementary age*. Give your child accurate and truthful information about the reproductive process. Decide on the names you'll use for body parts and processes.

Your public library or Christian bookstore should have books that guide you in talking to your child at every age level. Answer specific questions with specific facts. Don't try to strive for an in-depth response that gives your child more than he wants to know at the moment. Keep it simple.

2. *Preadolescence*. Contacts with pets and peers will give your child many occasions for questions. You'll need to correct misinformation and gently counter unhealthy peer attitudes. At the same time, a child needs to prepare for the changes that will take place in his or her body and emotions. Explain that sexual urges will be powerful. Listen to your child's ideas and attitudes about sex before giving him or her the facts. You can then best clear up the misconceptions he or she may have picked up from others and his or her own imaginings.

3. *Adolescence*. Point out the differences between male and female sexual urges. A girl should know that boys are primarily stimulated visually and are aroused much more quickly than girls. A boy should know that a girl's sexual urges are more frequently associated with romantic love and that his advances will easily

be interpreted as evidence of enduring love.

If you feel discomfort in discussing sex, be honest with your youngster. Make it clear that the subject is legitimate, but that your past training is responsible for your lack of ease. Learning and practicing the names of sexual organs and functions beforehand can help.

Work hard at keeping open, easy communication with your child. Make active, empathetic listening your goal. Avoid lectures like the plague. Your youngster's sense that you understand his or her predicaments is invaluable.

If your child should fail at sexual control, point him or her to the forgiveness available in Jesus Christ. Make sure you forgive as well. In adolescence, when sexual urges and peer pressure are intense, the best insulation against indiscriminate sexual behavior is a high degree of self-worth.

Obviously, a great variety of factors affect how your youngster will handle his or her sexuality. Your prayers and commitment to intelligent, sensitive, and balanced parenting can give your child the healthy view of sex he or she deserves and needs.

Are Family Traditions Worth the Effort?

Traditions are the threads from which our most valued memories are woven. According to social scientists who study the family, traditions make a significant difference in our lives by creating and reinforcing emotional security in the home. In fact, some studies have shown that the families with the strongest ties have the most traditions, and that ritual is a symbol of how family members feel about one another.

WHAT CUSTOMS CAN DO FOR YOUR FAMILY

Actually, customs can strengthen families in a number of ways. First of all, traditions establish continuity. They tie the present to the past, linking one year to the next and bridging the generations.

Family stability is another benefit of traditions. The regular, familiar patterns of consistent family customs — whether nightly bedtime stories or table grace before every meal — add a predictability to the cycle of family life that's both comfortable and comforting.

Some Tried and True Ideas

On birthdays, why not gather the family first thing in the morning around the birthday person's bed for a rousing rendition of the birthday song? Then decorate his or her place at the breakfast table with balloons, crepe paper, and cards.

For wedding anniversaries, take a family portrait or photo each year in front of the very same background as a record of the family's growth.

Christmas offers a whole season full of warm tradition possibilities. One idea is to choose a significant family event from the past twelve months that you'd like to remember. Then make or purchase a tree ornament that symbolizes the event. A toy kitten, for example, could represent a new pet, or a tiny boat, this year's vacation. Be sure to paint or carve the

Yet another reward of traditions is the sense of family identity they cultivate. Children today are constantly pressured by the media to identify with their peers instead of their families. But special customs at home help make a family unique and give its members a feeling of belonging.

Closely related to this benefit is the spirit of family unity traditions build. Think, for example, of the warm closeness each person feels when family members are together for the tra-

year on each one. Years from now, your Christmas tree will be a family "history book."

At Thanksgiving, some families tell the story of the Pilgrims before the big meal. Then, as a small basket is passed around, each person drops in two kernels of dried corn and with each shares something he or she is most thankful for.

Remember that traditions don't have to be yearly events. A good *weekly custom* is for Dad to give Mom a rest by preparing Sunday breakfast with help from the kids. And bedtimes and mealtimes are perfect moments for *daily traditions.*

These ideas should be starters to help you think of some traditions that are perfectly suited to your family. With a little imagination and preparation, family traditions will become family treasures.

ditional Thanksgiving dinner. Traditions cultivate a sense of oneness that endures even long after the children are grown and have moved away.

Finally, traditions enrich our lives with meaning by setting aside the average routine and focusing on what's important to us. It's easy to let normal days slip by unnoticed—but when we observe special days and events, we have a chance to pause and reflect on our lives. Birthdays, for example, remind us of the growth and uniqueness of each family member; wedding anniversaries call attention to the deepening love in marriage. And holidays such as Christmas, Easter, and Memorial Day give us opportunities to think about our faith and values, and to share them with our children.

In all these respects, you can strengthen your home by strengthening your traditions.

RX FOR TIRED TRADITIONS

If you find that one of your traditional observances has lost its meaning, or if you want to start some new ones, begin by asking your family these questions: First, what traditions have been carried on from the generations before us? (You may want to involve the grandparents in answering this one.) Next, how did our family's new traditions develop? And third, what new traditions would we like to add? Or, perhaps, what old ones would we like to re-establish?

Then, as you evaluate together your present traditions and plan new ones, keep these guidelines in mind:

- Remember that simple customs are best. Elaborate or expensive rituals can become difficult to maintain.
- Plan and prepare well ahead of time — sometimes weeks or even months. This builds anticipation that's also an important part of the fun. Avoid canceling or changing traditions on the spur of the moment.
- Choose traditions that focus on values and people rather than costly gifts or activities.

- Make sure every family member is included in both the preparation and the observance.
- Don't be pressured or rigid — enforcing a tradition takes the fun out of it. If an idea doesn't work, try a different one next time.
- Use the time as a "teachable moment" to call attention to the significance of the occasion. What better time to tell your children about God's love than on Christmas Eve? Or how about talking with teens about romance and marriage on your anniversary?
- Finally, if your family's ready to add some new traditions, ideas can come from many sources. Talk to grandparents and older relatives, especially if they're from "the old country." Ask other families what traditions they observe and why. Look for ideas in the novels you read or movies you watch. You can even check out library books on customs in other lands.

CHAPTER 6

*Give Your Child
Spiritual Values*

It is God's design that parents communicate true spiritual values to their children. What kinds of values are being modeled on the stage of your family life? Your children won't catch something you don't have.

St. Paul's words in 2 Timothy 3:14-15 indicate that our real goal is the third of three stages of spiritual development. The first is *knowledge* (reliable information about God). The second is *learning* (personal application of those truths). And the third is *wisdom* (a pattern of seeing from God's point of view). Parents who are successful at helping their children arrive at stage three are generally active in several key areas. Let's first take a personal inventory and then look at some practical suggestions.

A Personal Inventory

- Is my own spiritual life worth imitating? Do I pray privately for the specific needs of my family?
- Do I have a natural enthusiasm for spiritual things, or are prayer, Bible study, and church activities merely rote or optional habits?
- Is the way I discipline my child creating in him or her a balanced respect for authority that will help the child willingly respond to God's authority?
- Do I take my child to the Scriptures to discuss his or her problems, positive character traits being acquired, world events that concern the child, or questions about life?
- Is prayer joined with action my natural response when my child comes to me with needs? Does he or she see me take problems before God first? Does our family pray together naturally and spontaneously at other than mealtimes or bedtimes?

DEVELOPING SPIRITUAL AWARENESS
Psychological studies indicate that about 85 percent of your child's adult personality has been formed by his or her sixth birthday. So your best chance for success is to love and discipline your child effectively during those first crucial years. Then, as you work on the re-

maining 15 percent, here are some suggestions:

- If you've never dedicated your child to God by name, do it now. Give your child to him and recognize that he or she is only in your keeping for a season of time.
- Build in your home a balanced climate of laughter, adventure, surprises, mutual care, good music and books, and good friends. Make it fun to live there. One test of your home's atmosphere is whether the neighborhood kids like to congregate there!
- Pray for your child daily. Stay aware of his or her specific needs so that you can pray specifically. Let the child know you pray for him or her. Be sure to point out God's answers to prayer in the child's life. Pray often for his or her future concerns as well, such as vocations, spouse, and children.
- Treat your child's questions about spiritual matters seriously. Don't laugh if he or she wants to know if mosquitoes go to heaven; use the question as a chance to talk about our promised eternal life in God's presence. If you don't know an answer, say so; then go to the Bible or your pastor together for further insight.
- Have frequent times of spiritual interaction as a family, tailored to the interests and attention spans of your children. Get them involved in contributing. Change the pace frequently. Reward children for memorizing Scripture.
- Have times of spontaneous family worship. When a happy event calls for celebration,

thank God in songs and prayer together.

- Involve your child in an effective Christian summer camping program and any good scouting or youth program your church sponsors.
- Take advantage of holidays and other special occasions to talk about your faith. What better time to discuss God's love than on Christmas Eve, or his power than on Easter morning? Even birthdays can become occasions for emphasizing the uniqueness and worth in God's eyes of the person being honored, and wedding anniversaries are a natural time to discuss God's plan for marriages.
- Help your child become familiar and comfortable with your church—its members, order of worship, and activities.
- Expose your child to biographies of great Christian men and women and to contemporary Christian music.
- Hang a world map on your wall and study regularly the areas of hunger, political repression, and spiritual need. Write to mission groups for materials that tell what God is doing in various countries.
- Invite missionaries and spiritually committed people into your home. Encourage your child to ask questions to learn how God called these people.
- On a family bulletin board, post pictures of missionaries you have met. Correspond with them. Pray and give as a family to help meet their needs. Let your child help write the monthly checks.

- On your family vacation visit a missions out-reach or inner city ministry in the area where you're going.
- Identify friends of your child who do not know how to have a relationship with Christ. Pray and plan ways to spend time with them that might give you an opportunity to share the Christian message. Make sure you and your child know what to say when the opportunity arises.
- During your child's teenage years, his or her faith must become able to stand independently from yours. A teenager will likely begin questioning much of what he or she has previously accepted. Don't panic. Pray and provide exposure both to literature that gives solid answers to his or her questions, and to speakers who communicate well with young people. Be open to calm discussion yourself, and more than ever, practice what you preach.

In Proverbs 22:6, God promises you can give your child a heart for him. It's an ongoing process of mutual growth each day that will have immediate joys — and eternal rewards.

Why Chores, Children, and Character Go Together

With today's labor-saving devices, parents may wonder about the value of chores. But assigning chores has the distinction of being a most productive way of teaching responsibility and accountability to children. In our industrialized society, most children are no longer able to learn adult work skills by joining their parents on the job (such as working in the fields). Most adult activities are too technically complicated for children to help, and the workplace is far from home.

The home, however, can still be a place for learning skills that accomplish genuine work. The result is the development of valuable qualities such as diligence and perseverance, as well as a sense of satisfaction in the child. And as he or she begins to build competence, along with it will come self-confidence.

In addition, there are several educational benefits to teaching younger children domestic skills. Counting and arithmetic games, for example, can take place while washing dishes; sorting silverware helps them acquire sophisticated matching skills; and setting the table teaches right from left. In fact, almost all chores help a child learn to follow directions and carry out activities with several steps in sequence—an important foundation for many other educational skills.

Before helping your child develop character through chores, you and your spouse need to discuss some basics.

1. How you perceive the division of labor between male and female roles needs clear definition.

2. A high view of family democracy should underpin the plan you establish and enforce.

3. Recognize that while the child may not perform the work up to your standards at first, the main goal is his or her growth and improvement through the process.

4. Whatever strategy you have for assigning chores, it's bound to be frustrated eventually without regular and solid family communication.

HOW TO BUILD CHARACTER THROUGH CHORES

- Start early. A three-year-old can pick up toys and learn other skills such as making beds and putting dirty clothes in the hamper or clean clothes in drawers. A five-year-old can set tables, dust, dry dishes, even vacuum (though you'll have to help with corners). A chore may take three times as long when the child does it, but he or she will take great delight in accomplishing "real grown-up work."

- Don't discourage volunteers. Between the ages of eight and twelve, children go through an especially helpful period when they want to model their parents.
- Consider, when possible, the interests and abilities of your child in your assignments. Children take great pride in getting good at something they want to do.
- Divide and rotate the less desirable and the most popular tasks. Do this equally among all the family members.
- Spell out each task in writing, and make clear the standard of performance for a job well done. Leaving this up to individual interpretation creates problems. At the same time, give tips for accomplishing each task better, faster, and more easily.
- Create and display a chart where assignments and performances are logged.
- Don't spare the praise. If you spend more time criticizing a poorly done job than praising a good one, you've actually rewarded the negative behavior more than the positive performance. Lavish compliments are fun to give and never hurt anyone.
- Only extraordinary chores an outsider would normally be hired to perform deserve some pay. (An allowance is a better way to meet a child's regular need for some money.)
- Use chores to create and support a sense of family uniqueness and tradition. Adopt slogans such as, "We cooperate to make things work for everyone," and, "In our home rights and responsibilities are shared by all."

- Involve everyone in planning a chores system. List the various tasks and problems that arise with each, and talk about why everyone needs to share the load. Remember that children carry out duties and accept penalties they have helped set for themselves much more readily than those that are imposed upon them.
- From time to time help your child do the designated chores. He or she will see an attitude of servanthood in you worth imitating, and the work will provide a natural context for conversation and sharing.

Through it all, aim for fairness—the key to developing the mature sense of responsibility and accountability you want for your child. Yes, chores can be both fun and rewarding!

Dealing with Death

Dealing with death has never been easy, but in a culture that worships youthfulness, learning to cope with death is especially difficult. Mature models are scarce. And for children who are just beginning to learn about death, the loss of a pet, relative, or friend is a traumatic and bewildering experience.

The best way to help a child cope with bereavement will depend on several factors, including the child's age, the closeness to the child of the person who died, and the circumstances of death. Before you can help your child, however, you need to be aware of your own response to the event.

Grief is usually experienced in several stages, both by children and adults. In particular, we need to be aware that no matter how strong our faith in God, we're likely to experience stages of denial and anger that must be faced and overcome rather than repressed. Though we shouldn't hide these feelings from our children—they need to know that we feel them, too—we should depend on other adults to act as sounding boards and to help us work out our acceptance of the event. A child should never be put in the role of counselor.

A GUIDE TO GRIEVING
- A young child may ask questions about death when a pet or relative dies. These questions should be answered as honestly as possible, without either evasiveness or unnecessary details. A young child is apt to respond to the death of someone close by feeling guilty, because the child may remember being angry at the deceased and thus reason that the death is his or her fault. The child must be helped to realize that his feelings had no relationship to the event. He should also be helped to overcome feelings of rejection— that the close loved one intentionally abandoned him.
- If the death took place as a result of illness or in a hospital, care should be taken not to allow the child to form a close association between death and sickness. Otherwise the child may experience deep fears whenever he or she is ill or in the hospital. Small children should not be told that death is a sleep from which the deceased will never awake. Many children who've been told this develop a fear of going to sleep at night.
- Whether or not a small child should go to a funeral is debated; children over five or six are better able to understand and handle the experience. During the period following a death, the child should remain in the home

42

even though the parents are displaying grief. A child feels grief, and he or she needs to see others grieving as well.

- At about eight years of age, a child begins to understand the inevitability and irreversibility of death. At this point, he or she needs the freedom to bring up and discuss the subject. Avoid ridicule or shame and be sensitive to the child's fears. Uncertainty, aggression, and shyness are often expressions of fear at this age.

- A good experience is to include your child in a memorial service. Prepare him or her by talking about each part of the service, and point out that its purpose is to allow family and friends to recognize the good things about a person's life. If there is an open-casket review, let the child choose whether he or she will look or touch.

- An adolescent is better able to understand the full implications of dying and the finality of death. In a period already full of emotional turmoil, a teenager needs room to express feelings freely without judgment. The young person may desire privacy to sort out his or her thoughts, and may turn to other adults or even peers for emotional support.

- At any age, your child needs to understand death as well as he or she can in the context of faith. The Bible teaches that death is universal (Ps. 89:48, Heb. 9:27), a result of sin (Rom. 6:23, James 1:15), and an enemy (Luke 22:39-44, Matt. 26:36-44, 1 Cor. 15:26). In facing death, Christians grieve, but not without hope (1 Thess. 4:13). By

your example, encourage your child to acknowledge to God any feelings of anger, fear,
or rejection. And soothe those feelings by
remembering God's promises, his caring
presence, and his unconditional love.
- Agree with your child that everything that
happens in life does not always seem fair or
consistent. A realistic attitude will relieve
him or her of any guilt in feeling responsible
for the loss.
- Cherish together the promises in Psalms
23:4 and 116:15. The unknown is a fearful
thing, but believers are promised an escort
(John 14:1-3) and a resurrection (1 Cor.
15:51-52, 1 Thess. 4:13-18). We adults
cannot fully understand death, but we can
learn to trust God in the face of it.

Though God's presence in sorrow is im-
mensely encouraging, it does not eliminate
grief. We are still human. In your example of
freely trusting and facing the uncertainties of
life, your child will learn that it is OK to hurt,
and that our true feelings can be acknowledged
and expressed without shame. In helping your
child learn to cope with death, you'll be setting
him or her free to enjoy life.

How to Teach Honesty

Honesty is one of the "core values," the real stuff of integrity and personal maturity. Like other values, it cannot be laid on a child like a coat of paint. Instead, it grows like grain in wood—part of the total development. Our task as parents is to guide our children toward a strong conscience, a commitment to truth, and the ability to think for themselves.

THREE WAYS TO TEACH HONESTY

Teaching honesty involves three levels of instruction: (1) the factual, (2) the relational, and (3) the personal.

- The *factual* level is the ongoing process of storing in your child's mind the concept of honesty and the consequences of dishonesty. Bible stories that illustrate the value of integrity are useful.
- A child's psychosexual identity begins forming about the age of two. In addition to hearing what you say, he or she begins modeling

you more closely. This desire to imitate begins the *relational* level of instruction. Consequently you'll need to look carefully at your own standards of honesty. Even a young child observes and understands much more than you realize about your commitment to integrity. What are you saying to your teenager, for example, by your business ethics and methods of reporting income for taxes? Do you ever tell "little white lies" to flatter someone or to avoid a small inconvenience (such as having a child tell a telephone caller you're not home)?

It's also important that your child see you honestly admitting to your own failures; for example, driving too fast in hazardous conditions, not arriving home when you said you would, or not keeping a promise. Such realistic modeling frees the child to struggle with his or her own honesty problems.

One parent said that his kindergartner would never confess his sins to God in his bedside prayers until his dad began to confess openly his own shortcomings.

● The third level of training is to help the child *personalize* the principle of honesty in an everyday context. Show a preschooler or primary child a one-dollar bill and ask what he or she would do with it if it were found on the floor or mistakenly given back in change by a sales clerk. Emphasize that being honest makes one feel good, helps others, and pleases God as well as Mom and Dad. Role-play together other situations that would call for a decision to act honestly.

LEARNING RIGHT AND WRONG—
A PROCESS

Preschool. According to research, a child in the earliest years has no internalized sense of right or wrong, only a fear of consequences. The child accepts what parents say because he or she wants to please. Praise versus a spanking or confinement to his or her room is the child's measure of an honest action, so ethical reasoning will have little effect on the behavior of a young child.

Elementary age. Now the child's conscience has begun to mature, and actions are judged by internal moral standards. At this age honesty can be taught by telling true-to-life stories. Ask, for example, what the child would do if he or she saw a friend slip a candy bar into his lunch sack while in a grocery store. Follow with questions such as "Why?" and "What would result?"

By this age, most children should have moved beyond the motivation of merely pleasing parents, and should be doing right things because it also makes the child happy with him or herself.

Adolescence. By the time they reach preadolescence and adolescence, most children have a well-developed conscience. They should be thinking at more abstract levels about the values they hold. You can encourage this by discussing with your teenager newspaper articles that report various acts of dishonesty, both by individuals and by groups in business and government. Help your teenager discern the motivations for such acts.

THREE TIPS FOR TRUTHFUL KIDS

- Role-play realistic situations appropriate to your child's age — the temptation to cheat on exams, use someone else's I.D. card, or lie to parents about where he or she has been are examples. Speculate about the consequences of dishonesty, especially the damage it does to relationships. Note how one lie often leads to another in order to cover it up. Guide your child to see that without honesty, we can't get along with others in a healthy way — whether in school, home, marriage, community, or government.

- Give your child a strong sense of honesty rooted in Scripture. In this way, he or she will rise above the frequent trap of seeing right and wrong only in terms of what is most pleasurable, approved by others, or most expedient. The child's conscience will be sensitive to dishonesty in all its forms and will help him or her consistently avoid it.

- Focus on your child's actions as well as those of others. Affirm and praise the child, both alone and in front of his or her peers. Putting an honest label on your child will underscore that value and motivate him or her to live up to it when faced with the genuinely tough choices of life.

Your Child and Stress

Stress. Anyone alive in this shaky, competitive, fast-paced world of ours experiences a good deal of it, including our children. A child's life may seem carefree compared to that of a corporate executive—but children suffer from stress just as adults do. Only the symptoms are different.

A child's equivalent of the executive ulcer can be anything from frequent colds to reading problems. Behavioral symptoms often involve:

- withdrawal
- a decrease in verbal expression
- unusually aggressive behavior

Physical responses might include:

- diarrhea
- itching
- skin problems
- a change in eating habits
- nightmares

Studies show a high correlation between continuing stress into adulthood and health problems such as high blood pressure, heart disease, and cancer. It is important that children develop good patterns for dealing with stress.

Stress is basically wear and tear on the body. Some stress is normal and necessary for healthful living. It keeps the mind agile and the circulatory system functioning. It also spurs us to do well on exams, to compete better in athletic events, to love and cry and strive for a more satisfying life.

But when stress becomes distress, the problems in health and behavior begin. The possible sources of unhealthy stress in children are many, including events such as a move to a new town, a chronic illness, the birth of a sibling, or the loss of a loved one. Stress may originate internally as a result of faulty relationships or destructive behavior. Or it may stem from some external and uncontrollable situation or event.

How can we help children lessen the sources of stress and cope with the stress that will still be inevitable? The way you handle stress as a parent will set an example for your child. Here are some approaches for both you and your child to consider.

FIFTEEN WAYS TO ALLEVIATE STRESS

- Talk about it. One of the worst responses to stress is to hold it in—to feel that you're alone in facing the problem. Create opportunities for a young child to express his or her emotions. Playing with hand puppets and drawing are good activities in this regard.

- Be sensitive to the child's comments that might be clues to anxiety. As a child grows older, he or she is more able to identify and analyze frustrations. A mention of the school bully or the divorce of a friend's parents may be the time for some gentle questioning to bring hidden fears out into the open where they can be overcome.

- Visualize possible solutions together. Help your child identify specific actions he or she can take to resolve a stressful situation. If the problem, for example, is his or her falling behind in school, talk about how the child can better schedule time, improve study habits, use your help, or obtain more help from teachers.
- When an interpersonal relationship in your child's life is involved, help him or her assess where responsibility for the problem lies. The child may wrongly be taking responsibility for another's actions over which he or she has no control.
- Check out God's Word on a problem. One of the great privileges of Christians is that we can cast our cares upon the Lord, and receive genuine peace and rest in return (Rom. 8:26-28). Honest prayer can relieve stress. Pray with your child. Simple obedience may be the proper solution if he or she is violating one of God's principles for living.
- Live one day at a time. Most of the things both children and adults worry about never happen. A focus on the here and now can be healthy. Sometimes we just need to enjoy the present moment and postpone dealing with the source of stress until a more appropriate time. Suggest to your child that he or she not worry about a problem until you

can talk about it together in a relaxed setting.
- Allow your child adequate time for play. It's one of the most important channels a child has for dealing with stress. Invest in toys that give the greatest scope to the child's imagination and creativity, such as clay, blocks, or woodcarving tools.
- Make sure everyone in your family gets adequate sleep and exercise.
- Limit the amount of TV your child watches. Too much TV watching results in stress from informational and emotional overload.
- Don't use your child as a therapist. A single parent is especially tempted to unload problems on children because no other adult is in the home. Find a relative, close friend, or clergyman to listen instead.
- Set realistic goals for your child. Avoid pushing him or her into athletic, academic, or artistic competition, or setting unrealistic goals for achievement.
- Arrange, if possible, for each child to have his or her own private space. Even if it is just the corner of a room, it's important to have a place to be alone.
- Set aside a regular "quiet time." Unplug the radio, TV, and even the phone!
- Share relaxing moments with your child. Stop to watch a sunset, examine a flower, admire a birdsong.
- Finally, laugh a lot together! The healing power of laughter has long been recognized as an effective antidote for stress.

What to Do about Criticism

It is a secure and mature person who can receive criticism and calmly evaluate it. Even wiser is the one who can give criticism in a constructive and winsome way. Wiser still is the parent who can develop these qualities in children.

Few other skills can better promote strength of character, healthy self-esteem, and stability throughout the storms and inequities of life. But even though the role of critic is an ancient and respected one, talking about criticism is tough. Too often criticism degenerates into condemnation. No wonder Scripture gives us guidelines to help keep us from becoming condemning critics. The best-known warning of all, spoken by Jesus himself, is: "Pass no judgment, and you will not be judged. For as you judge others, so you will yourself be judged, and whatsoever measure you deal out to others will be dealt back to you" (Matt. 7:1, NEB).

Scripture also instructs: "Therefore, putting away falsehood, let everyone speak the truth with his neighbor, for we are members one of another" (Eph. 4:25, RSV).

HOW TO CRITICIZE CONSTRUCTIVELY
- Criticize the action rather than the person.
- Don't criticize in anger. You'll usually overreact.
- Don't criticize when you're fatigued or under some other stress. Wait until your mind is clear and your mood is positive.
- Get all the facts — every situation has at least two sides.
- Give criticism in love, clearly and thoughtfully. Choose words that aren't emotionally charged. Absolutes like *always* and *never* hurt and usually exaggerate the truth.
- Don't criticize by comparing the person with someone else. In particular, don't compare siblings with each other, and *never* compare your spouse unfavorably with one of your parents.
- Often the things that irritate us the most in others are the faults we have ourselves. "Why do you see the speck that is in your brother's eye, but do not notice the log that is in your own eye?" (Matt. 7:3, RSV). Before you criticize a specific habit or trait, ask yourself if you have the same problem!
- Try to include a positive alternative to the negative action, attitude, or habit you're criticizing.

HOW TO RECEIVE CRITICISM CONSTRUCTIVELY
- Receiving criticism is most difficult when we mistakenly feel that what we *do* is the same thing as what we *are*.

- Always consider the source when deciding how much weight should be given to a criticism.
- Give the person a chance to finish what he or she is saying before you attempt a response.
- The best immediate response to criticism is to attempt to clarify. Make a statement such as, "What I hear you saying is. . . ." Don't react with self-defense.
- When the criticism is justified thank the person and, if necessary, ask his or her forgiveness.

FAMILY EXERCISES

To help your children learn how to give and receive criticism, try these exercises:

- Participate with your child in a little self-criticism, being sensitive to how much your youngster's self-image can tolerate. Set the pace by confessing some way you fail as a parent. Invite your child's comments and reactions. Ask your child to identify one of his or her own failures. Make constructive suggestions to each other, pray together, and promise your mutual support in these specifics.
- Talk about the value of seeking out constructive criticism from others, especially from a trusted friend. Discuss some occasions when you've done this and how it helped.
- Help your child understand ways he or she can deal with the destructive criticism the child receives from peers and authority

figures. One useful response is to acknowledge that the criticism has been heard without responding to it. This may sound something like, "I'm sorry you feel that I. . . ." Another effective response is to assume for a moment that the speaker may have some truth in what he or she is saying and agree. Such a dialogue might go something like this:

"You did a terrible job!"

"Yes, I probably could have done that better."

"You certainly could have. That was awful!"

"Yes, it really looks bad, doesn't it?"

About this point, most critics begin to run out of things to say, and their tension is defused.

- Stage a family discussion about criticism and do some role-playing. Talk first about the principles of criticism we've discussed, then make a game of giving and receiving critical comments. Use the response techniques mentioned above. Begin with simple situations, and watch for violations of the principles. Help the person rephrase his or her words. Practice like this can help form new patterns of response when it's no longer just a game.

Most of all, remember to practice what you preach. How blessed is the parent or the child who has loyal critics and knows how to receive their help!

Will Your Child Make Good Choices?

Did you know that the decisions you made today were rooted in your own self-concept—that image developed over sixteen to eighteen years of growing up in your parents' home? How you view your ability to perform in relation to others substantially affects your decision making.

For that reason, helping children learn to make wise choices involves both teaching them an adequate process and helping them develop a healthy self-image of competence.

BASIC DECISION-MAKING PROCESSES

Although decision-making systems vary, the basic processes involved are:

- defining the decision to be made
- selecting the best option
- accepting and assessing the consequences

As a parent, your task is to model, guide, and support your child's developing competence in these processes, a job that will change as your child grows older.

Preschool. A preschooler sees you in a god-like role. He or she needs you to be directive without being dictatorial. You should help guide both the definition and selection phases of decision making. The child's greatest growth will occur as he or she realizes consequences and begins to apply what has been learned from past decisions. For example, you may be helping him or her decide which of two pairs of shoes is most appropriate to wear in cold or wet weather.

Elementary age. Now your child closely models you as his or her hero. At this stage, the child's participation in the selection process should increase. You can reinforce a positive self-concept by helping the child master certain tasks and develop a pattern of good choices in recurring decisions. How he or she spends after-school hours is a good opportunity to practice decision making.

Preadolescence. At this stage, children are beginning to sense that parents have both strengths and weaknesses. A child's privacy and peer relationships will begin to divert more and more of his or her attention. So try to include the child's friends in some family activities. Help the preadolescent broaden significantly in decision-making skills by allowing him or her to assume responsibility to define alternatives and anticipate consequences.

Make your comments as illustrative as the child's maturity and wisdom will allow. Showing him or her how to list on paper the pros and cons of more complex decisions would be a good exercise.

Six Steps to Making a Good Decision

1. Determine what needs to be decided.
2. Determine what the options are. Consider every possible way the decision could be made. Go beyond the obvious alternatives and consider more creative solutions. At this point, don't consider how "way out" the ideas may be; this is the time for brainstorming, and sometimes a crazy idea can lead to a practical one. Write down all ideas.
3. Think about the strengths and weaknesses of each choice. Consider pros and cons and determine what is feasible and what is not. Search for all the possible consequences of each choice.
4. Choose the best alternative. If this first choice doesn't work out, make a second choice in the same way the first was made.
5. Do what you've decided to do.
6. Evaluate the decision after you've seen the results. Decide whether or not it was a good choice, and whether you'd make the same decision if you had to choose again.

Adolescence: This is often the time of rebellious activity and tension. Be supportive as your child struggles to redefine himself. Encourage the teenager to build skills and develop

More Tips on Decision-Making

Joy Berry suggests three guidelines for the child to keep in mind in making every decision:
1. Do everything you can to show God your love for him.
2. Do everything you can to take care of yourself.
3. Do everything you can to show others you care.

For an excellent book to help children in decision making and problem solving, see Berry's *Making Up Your Own Mind* (Word, 1978).

talents rather than roles. Focus your attention on helping your child to clarify and define the decisions that must be made instead of evaluating the quality of his or her choices. Having to face the consequences of his own poor choices will be far more instructive than your strong words. The next stage will be complete independence.

A good exercise for all ages is to role-play a "what if" scene. Set up an imaginary situation — as common or unusual as you like — and ask, "What if this happened to you? What would you do?" Then go through the decision-making process together. Try situations like these: What if you missed your bus stop and found yourself in a strange section of the city without money for a phone call? What if your best friend asked you to help him or her cheat on a math test? What if someone asked you to marry him/her? What if you were graduating from high school and had to choose a college?

Throughout the process of learning to make decisions, don't force or even encourage leap-frogging of the stages. It will only frustrate your child and require relearning later. Be a positive model in the way you approach decisions in the family. Your child will be watching. Admit your mistakes and celebrate your successes. And remember, your basic assignment as a parent is to work yourself out of a job.

Give Your Child a Thankful Spirit

You know the feeling that comes to you when someone—your child or a colleague—comes to you with a warm "thank you" for something you've done. It's the same feeling you have when your little "angel," with face beaming and eyes sparkling, comes bounding in from her first thrilling ride on the new swing set you bought her. "Oh, thank you, Mommy!" she squeals as her small arms squeeze around your neck. Or when your teenage son slaps you on the back and says, "Thanks, Dad, for letting me use the car. You're really OK."

You also know the embarrassment you feel when profound silence follows a gift you've given your child or someone else. Or your deep disappointment when a favor you've just performed goes completely unacknowledged.

What went wrong? What does it take to build a consistent and spontaneous spirit of genuine thankfulness in our children?

HOW TO BUILD AN ATTITUDE OF GRATITUDE

Be sensitive enough to require only that each child act his age in the way thanks is expressed.

Your Behavior: More Important Than You Think

- Research has indicated that nothing influences children's value systems more than the relationship they observe between their mom and dad. So how often and how openly does your child see you and your spouse expressing your appreciation to each other?
- Frequent expression of your appreciation for who your child is and what he or she does can also stimulate a thankful spirit. Did you know that as the child feels more secure in your appreciation and approval, he or she will express personal thankfulness to others more freely?

It's also important to recognize that true thankfulness cannot be demanded. Making your child feel guilty for not feeling thankful doesn't accomplish much. A better approach is to look for the underlying message in his or her unthankful spirit. What do you hear? Insecurity, fear, anger, revenge seeking, or a desperate reach for attention might be what your child is giving vent to. And if you can hear the message and meet the need, a thankful spirit will soon be restored. The child will appreciate you for that kind of unconditional love.

There are some specific things you can do to build thankfulness in children of various ages. Here are a few:

Preschool. Children this age are naturally very self-centered. Most thanking at this age is done to gain approval for being good. Give your approval freely, and openly thank your child and God for the child's specialness.

Try playing with your little one the "Thank You, Body" game. Take turns thanking your body parts for their respective functions, such as "Thank you, hands, for helping me eat."

Elementary age. Children at this stage can make creative expressions of thankfulness. Help your child express gratitude to other family members by writing simple songs or poems on special occasions such as birthdays, Mother's and Father's Day, and Valentine's Day.

Make a family tradition of giving homemade thank-you cards. Take a few minutes from time to time to create together a simple card or note for any number of small favors.

Occasionally, have the family compose together a thank-you letter to someone who has been a help to you. It could be a grandparent, perhaps, or a baby-sitter or teacher. Think how the mail carrier would feel to find a thank-you note and a bag of cookies in the mailbox especially for him or her!

Preadolescence. Gift-giving and helping projects are particularly important expressions of thankfulness for this age group. A child this age has a greater ability to respond to other people's needs. And when in return the child's own needs are met, he or she will readily identify with the pleasure of saying thank you.

Adolescence. Here's another time of strong self-centeredness. The young person is beginning to see himself even more as an individual who is different from others. Make sure you're giving emotional as well as material gifts to your teenager—gifts such as respect, trust, and personal time.

Regardless of the age of your children, make it a habit to express your thanks to God openly and spontaneously as a family. Make sure your family prayers begin with praise and thanksgiving before you make requests. Experience the joy of small things together with your child, such as the glory of the night sky or the happiness of a new puppy. Make the pleasure of these occasions complete with an unashamed, out-loud "Thank you, Lord!" And don't forget that even when things aren't going well, "Give thanks in all circumstances" (1 Thess. 5:18, NIV).

The Thanksgiving Game

The next time you have a few minutes to spare while riding in the car, try being thankful "from A to Z." Take turns thinking of things to be grateful for that begin with each letter of the alphabet. For example, "Thank you, Lord, for apples . . . angels . . . alligators . . . automobiles." Be flexible with hard letters like *X*. Use items like "X-cellent health" and "X-tra special friends."

Allowances and Financial Responsibility

Teaching children the wise stewardship of resources is essential, and training them how to handle money is a good place to start. One of the best ways for children to learn about money is to have an allowance.

Many parents do not give formal allowances, but instead give their children money on an irregular, unplanned basis as it is requested. This method doesn't teach them how to manage money. Children must beg for money, and the parent must continually decide on the spot whether each request is legitimate and affordable.

A regular allowance avoids these problems, but there are widely divergent opinions about which type of allowance is best. Some parents pay children only for chores done around the house. Others give a regular allowance but withhold it if chores are left undone or as punishment for misbehavior. Many parents, however, think these methods encourage children to be good only for the money, and to see household chores as paid labor instead of natural responsibilities as members of the family. At the same time, the irregularity of payment makes it impossible for children to learn how to budget or save their income.

Other parents pay allowances regularly at a fixed amount, with no conditions attached. This system seems best for helping children learn to budget, but it fails to teach the connection between work and rewards.

THE BEST ALLOWANCE

The best approach, perhaps, is a combination of the two methods above. Give each child a regular, fixed allowance that must be budgeted for specific basic needs, plus a little more to spend at his or her discretion. This allowance is simply the child's share of the income as a family member. At the same time, basic responsibilities around the house are expected to be fulfilled; if they aren't, take disciplinary measures other than withholding allowance.

In addition, extra chores you might normally pay someone else to do—like mowing the grass or washing the car—can be done by your child for additional earnings. This extra income will teach the connection between work and wages, and will be available to the child for "fun" things that aren't basic needs.

The effectiveness of such an allowance in building a solid sense of financial responsibility and values will depend to a great extent upon how much money is given and the guidelines you establish for its use. Here are some principles:

- The way you handle your own money is the strongest statement you will make, no matter what you say.
- Allowances should be paid regularly, on time, and without your having to be reminded. Regularity is the key to teaching discipline in spending.
- Advances on allowances should be rare. Give no more or less than what has been agreed upon so your child can learn to balance spending with income.
- The size of an allowance should be based on what the child is expected to accomplish with it, taking into consideration the child's age, readiness, and needs, plus the family's circumstances.
- Include a portion that can be spent however the child pleases so that he or she will learn how to make wise choices in spending.
- You are entitled to exercise some control to keep expenditures within the rules and values of the family.
- Don't use an allowance in place of your time or to "buy" love.

TEACHING FINANCIAL RESPONSIBILITY

Preschool. Begin by helping your preschooler learn to understand pennies, nickels, and dimes in the context of playing store. Giving your child some change to spend on an occasional shopping trip with you will make the point that money is a medium of exchange.

Elementary age. A young school-age child

can be responsible for such items as lunch money, toothpaste, family gifts, and socks. Teach the importance of setting aside a tithe first. Then help the child to itemize on a budget worksheet the fixed expenses for which he or she will be responsible, as well as discretionary expenses. Also insist on some fixed amount for savings, preferably toward a long-term goal.

Between the ages of seven and nine, most youngsters are ready to begin managing a weekly allowance using a budget worksheet. Items purchased with discretionary funds or savings will become especially important lessons in finance. As your child grows he or she can save toward larger purchases. A few poor choices with this saved money will quickly teach the importance of price versus value. Let your child learn the hard way: don't bail him or her out, and bite your tongue when you want to say, "I told you so."

Including a preteen in some family financial discussions is a good way for the child to learn that household income is limited, and that sometimes difficult decisions must be made about spending priorities. These family discussions can also become a good time for a child to learn about taxes, insurance, social security, and credit. Meanwhile, be sure that your child doesn't shoulder the weight of a financial crisis, or feel guilty about costing you money.

Adolescence. Remember that as a child grows, so does his or her need for money. A review of allowances twice a year is a good idea. A teenager should be encouraged to work outside the home, and this additional income should be deducted from the allowance so that the budget continues to balance. You can also help put a major purchase (such as a car) within reach and teach savings discipline by agreeing to put up one-half of the cost if the child will save the other half.

However you handle the details of allowances, remember: the best lesson your children learn about money will be your example. Are you modeling the priorities, values, and stewardship you want your youngsters to learn?

Helping Your Child Cope with Guilt

One of our goals as parents must be to help our children develop strong and healthy consciences. They must gain an understanding of guilt by learning the difference between the "fact" of guilt and the "feelings" of guilt. Feeling guilty does not always mean a real transgression has occurred.

An imbalanced perception of guilt may have one or two unhealthy results. A person may suffer from the oppression of a cruel, tyrannical superego that cannot distinguish between genuine and irrational guilt. Or the very opposite problem may result; he or she may be capable of doing wrong without any apparent feelings of guilt at all.

In training our children, it is important that they (as well as we) distinguish between factual guilt and false guilt. Both are usually accompanied by guilt feelings that are unpleasant. But guilt feelings from genuine guilt can motivate us to repent and be forgiven, while false guilt feelings only haunt and slowly destroy us.

FACTUAL GUILT OR FALSE GUILT?

1. *Factual guilt* is the result of an actual violation of civil or moral law—what the Bible calls sin.

2. Guilt feelings that come from one's failure to gain the approval or praise of others are the result of *false guilt*.

3. Feeling guilty for falling short of one's own unrealistic expectation is another kind of *false guilt*.

THREE CASE STUDIES

Too often children struggle unsuccessfully with persistent guilt feelings because they can't pinpoint the source of their guilt and thus can't deal properly with it. Each of the three kinds of guilt feelings described above requires a different approach.

When Mark comes home from junior high school feeling empty and sullen because he cheated on his math test, he's experiencing negative feelings from factual guilt. Mark's factual guilt will be removed when he admits to himself that what he did was clearly wrong, confesses it to God and then to his parents and/or teacher, becomes willing to take the consequences, and makes a personal commitment not to repeat the wrongdoing. In the Bible this is known as repentance, and each of these steps is necessary to remove the feelings of factual guilt.

When six-year-old Susie falls on the playground and feels rejected and stupid because her friends call her a baby for crying, that's false guilt. Young Susie's feelings of guilt for crying will go away when she is encouraged to give herself permission to cry when hurt, even if others do make fun of her. Children need to off-set their sensitivity to their peers' approval or rejection with a growing trust in their own per-ceptions and decisions.

Jimmy is ashamed and embarrassed because he struck out in the bottom of the ninth with the bases loaded. Jimmy's guilt feelings will vanish when he admits to his unrealistic expec-tations. He is his own worst critic and desper-ately needs from his parents unconditional love and acceptance that is not altered or lessened whenever performance is less than perfect. Unconditional loving, more than anything else, helps a child see himself as a special and valu-able creation of God.

COPING TIPS

How do you help your child gain a balanced skill in coping with his or her guilt?

- Avoid intensifying guilt by telling the child what a bad person he or she must be to have done such a terrible thing. Emphasize that the behavior is bad, not the person. "Hate the sin but love the sinner."
- Never withdraw your love and affection as a form of punishment. Let your love reflect God's love, which is unconditional despite our failings.
- Match the intensity of your discipline to the severity of the transgression, not to the in-tensity of your emotional displeasure. If you

must, give yourself time to cool off before administering correction.

- When disciplining, always provide a way for your child to retain his or her sense of value and dignity. Don't accompany correction with angry accusations or insults to the child's character or worth, such as, "You're just lazy!" or "You always make stupid mistakes!" And don't humiliate him or her in front of others.

- Structure your child's chores, responsibilities, limits, and rules in a way that optimizes his or her chances for success. Keeping the expectations in line with the child's level of maturity protects him or her from the tyranny of unrealistic goals and excessive disappointment.

- Be alert to reading materials, TV shows, movies, and real-life experiences that demonstrate healthy attitudes and solutions to guilt. Help your child understand the situational ethic, which underlies most of our culture's false view of right and wrong.

- When your child describes the misbehavior of a peer, capture the usefulness of the moment by asking, "Was that wrong? Why?" You'll gain a window on your child's thinking and understanding of guilt.

- Model in your own life a proper response to the three kinds of guilt feelings. When your child observes and confronts you with wrongdoing in your life, openly accept it as a golden moment of growth for both of you. Let him or her observe your repentance as well.

- Forgive your child and teach the art of forgiving others. This will also increase the child's capacity to forgive him or herself.

  You can give your child few greater gifts than an understanding of the sources of guilt and the ability to deal with them. Such a well-informed conscience will become the root of a happy, healthy life.

How to Build a Positive View of Authority

A recent bumper sticker declares, "Challenge Authority"—and many youths are doing just that. Concerned parents know that a child's attitudes and response patterns toward authority substantially impact his or her success, both now and as a future adult and parent. Building a balanced view isn't easy, but the following suggestions can help:

- Until the age of eight or nine, your youngster isn't capable of genuine abstract reasoning. His or her perceptions of authority are built from experience with parents and teachers, and the various rules of home, playground, and classroom.
- Build a positive view during these formative years by emphasizing fairness. Be as impartial as possible in the guidance and discipline you give. Fair discipline administered out of love builds self-esteem and will elicit a positive response. Arbitrary discipline, based on sheer power, tears down the child and provokes reaction.

- In making and enforcing family rules, regularly discuss their two-fold purpose: protection from making bad mistakes and harm, and provision for making life's relationships more enjoyable. Your best opportunities are found in daily experiences. Disputes among neighborhood kids, for example, afford an ideal opportunity to talk about the role of rules, who has "authority" to make or change them, and what happens when they're violated. If your child is along when you receive a traffic citation, use the opportunity to explain why traffic laws are essential for safety and why violators including yourself, must be prosecuted. Keep the focus on the protection and blessing that underlie rules and authority.
- Consider your own attitude toward authority. Do you speak respectfully of your child's teachers and principal, the police, and government officials even when you disagree with their decisions? Children naturally imitate their parents' attitudes toward authority.

FOUR SOURCES OF AUTHORITY

Help your child distinguish between various sources of authority:

1. *Absolute authority* is God's alone. He is our Creator, and there is no higher authority. Moral law begins with him. The laws of nature, for example, express his authority in the natural realm.

2. *Constitutional authority* derives from the

consensus of those people living democratically under its control. Government, public education, the military, police and fire protection, and other public officials, servants, and representatives, have authority only because that power has been given to them.

3. *Delegated authority* is that conferred by a higher power. A policeman can make an arrest only because he has been given authority by a higher law and power. A stop sign carries no intrinsic authority, but we obey it because it represents an authority over us.

As parents, our basic authority over our children is delegated by God. Take time to show your child in the Scriptures God's instructions to parents — for example, Ephesians 6:4. The resulting insight can help them better understand your actions and discipline.

4. Experience, character, and relationships are *other common sources of authority.* A person's advice is often valuable because he speaks from experience. The integrity and strength of a person's character can command authority. Jesus, for example, having set aside his divine power, still spoke with authority because of his personal character. And relationships often command authority. Witness how ruthlessly peer pressure modifies style of dress, speech, and a host of attitudes and behaviors in young people.

A positive view of authority built during your child's early years will help simplify your parenting when your adolescent begins internalizing his or her understanding of authority as a system of values and controls.

WHAT ABOUT REBELLION?

A certain amount of rebellion stems from the normal process of establishing independence. Some is our fault, if we have wielded authority over our child as a personal defense mechanism—gaining power at the expense of affirming our child's personhood and need to make his or her own choices. Here, rebellion is actually healthy because the issue is not submission, but rather the abuse of authority.

Other rebellion attempts to find its justification in rejecting society's values and appealing to different but carnal principles. Terrorism is a good example of this type of rebellion. The next time you view with your child a news report about terrorist activity, talk about the underlying view of authority. It could create a bridge for discussing what motivates rebellion in your child.

Giving your child a mature and balanced view of authority isn't easy, but little of real importance ever is. Success at it is certainly worth your effort!

Teaching Kids to Follow Through

Children play games "to the finish." So why do they find it hard to follow through with day-to-day tasks—a key to successful living? And how can parents help them gain this positive habit?

One hurdle to be overcome is that sticking with a task or skill until it's mastered isn't very popular today. We have a cultural bias toward the "instant fix" in foods, appliances, personal wants—even spirituality. Add to this the prevailing notion that society owes us a living, and it's obvious why kids aren't committed to perseverance.

THE SECRETS OF MOTIVATION

How can you help your child learn to follow through? Keep in mind these motivational principles:

Preschool. With a preschool child, balance is important. At this age, your child is motivated primarily by rewards or punishments and can't understand that a job must be completed because it's the "right" thing to do. When the child is failing to finish an assignment, it's best to pitch in and help. This modeling communicates your support and the importance you attach to finishing the task. It also avoids the discouragement and tension nagging brings.

Being sensitive to your youngster is critical. Low expectations won't challenge your child to reach his or her potential. Expectations set too high generate a devastating fear of failure.

One way to emphasize the right principle is to read popular children's stories that reinforce the value of persistence, like *The Little Engine That Could*. Older children would enjoy reading the biographies of famous persistent people, such as Thomas A. Edison (who had to persevere in developing such inventions as the light bulb) or Martin Luther King (who persevered in pressing for civil rights).

Elementary age. Your child's motivations will reach more of a reciprocal "back-scratching" stage. During this period increase both your support and your expectations. Introduce him or her to mottos such as, "If at first you don't succeed, try, try again," "Character is what you do on the third and fourth tries," and the moral of Aesop's tortoise and hare fable: "Slow and steady wins the race." You might underpin this with a discussion of the biblical principle of diligence. See Ecclesiastes 10:18, 11:6; Proverbs 10:4, 12:24, 13:4, and 22:29; Colossians 3:23; and 2 Thessalonians 3:11-13.

Remain lavish in your praise and reward outstanding efforts. Remind your child of occasions when he or she followed through and reaped the satisfaction of accomplishment.

When your child fails to finish, make clear both your disappointment and your total support and love. Once again, offering help when your child is seriously frustrated or ready to quit is the best way to show support and model the discipline needed. And a consistent example in keeping your own commitments to your children is most important.

Adolescence. In teen years, your child's motivations for following tasks should begin reflecting a more conscious and mature appreciation for the necessity of order in life. Expect your son or daughter to become consistent at basic chores, homework, taking care of possessions, and keeping promises. When the teenager fails, don't shield him or her from the resulting consequences. But don't remove your understanding love, and support, either.

KNOWING WHEN TO SAY "NO"

Of course, there's also a flip side to the discipline of following through. Sooner or later, all of us must give up on some things which we find to be beyond our abilities, overly demanding, or simply not enjoyable. So how does a child quit without becoming a quitter? Here are some principles to consider in forming the answer:

- Is there a natural quitting time? Can your child hold out until then? Sticking something out until the bitter end or until a natural cutoff point is a more positive choice than quitting at the moment of greatest stress, when difficulties are obscuring the end goal.

- Whose idea was the activity in the first place? If it wasn't your child's own choice, then abandoning it should be allowed more easily. If your child had begged to do it, be tougher.
- Was the commitment casually made? Help your child become fully aware of what may be involved in following through on a decision. This will yield a greater reluctance to give up when difficulties or fatigue arise.
- Are there exceptional circumstances in this case? Situations can change midstream. When your child wants to quit, ask lots of noncritical questions and listen "between the lines" for the negative factors discouraging him or her.
- Ask yourself, "Would it be called quitting if an adult were taking this action?"
- What will happen if the child isn't permitted to quit? Children need permission to back out when they've simply made a wrong choice, just as adults do. When we don't allow it, they adopt other undesirable behaviors, such as "forgetting," to cope with the pressure overload. It's better to help children behave responsibly while committed and then make a clean, honest, "I don't like it" or "I want out" break.

Your child can learn the discipline of following through. Few traits will be more important to his or her success as an adult—so don't neglect to follow through on this one!

Keeping Track

Child's name _____

Current age _____

Date of this record update _____

✔ = Current Area of Focus
/ = Successful Performance

(Circle Current Status)

Poor   Great
1 2   3   4   5   6   7   8   9   10

1. _____ Self-esteem
         1 2 3 4 5 6 7 8 9 10
2. _____ The art of friendship
         1 2 3 4 5 6 7 8 9 10
3. _____ Commitment to family
         1 2 3 4 5 6 7 8 9 10
4. _____ Learning about sex
         1 2 3 4 5 6 7 8 9 10
5. _____ Family traditions
         1 2 3 4 5 6 7 8 9 10
6. _____ A heart for God
         1 2 3 4 5 6 7 8 9 10
7. _____ Chores and responsibility
         1 2 3 4 5 6 7 8 9 10
8. _____ Dealing with death
         1 2 3 4 5 6 7 8 9 10
9. _____ Honesty
         1 2 3 4 5 6 7 8 9 10
10. _____ Handling stress
         1 2 3 4 5 6 7 8 9 10
11. _____ Giving and receiving criticism
         1 2 3 4 5 6 7 8 9 10

12. _____ Making good decisions
1 2 3 4 5 6 7 8 9 10

13. _____ A thankful spirit
1 2 3 4 5 6 7 8 9 10

14. _____ Allowances and financial
responsibility
1 2 3 4 5 6 7 8 9 10

15. _____ Coping with guilt
1 2 3 4 5 6 7 8 9 10

16. _____ A positive view of authority
1 2 3 4 5 6 7 8 9 10

17. _____ Learning to follow through
1 2 3 4 5 6 7 8 9 10

Child's name _____

Current age _____

Date of this record update _____

✔ = Current Area of Focus
/ = Successful Performance

(Circle Current Status)

Poor   Great
1   2   3   4   5   6   7   8   9   10

1. _____ Self-esteem
       1   2   3   4   5   6   7   8   9   10
2. _____ The art of friendship
       1   2   3   4   5   6   7   8   9   10
3. _____ Commitment to family
       1   2   3   4   5   6   7   8   9   10
4. _____ Learning about sex
       1   2   3   4   5   6   7   8   9   10
5. _____ Family traditions
       1   2   3   4   5   6   7   8   9   10
6. _____ A heart for God
       1   2   3   4   5   6   7   8   9   10
7. _____ Chores and responsibility
       1   2   3   4   5   6   7   8   9   10
8. _____ Dealing with death
       1   2   3   4   5   6   7   8   9   10
9. _____ Honesty
       1   2   3   4   5   6   7   8   9   10
10. _____ Handling stress
       1   2   3   4   5   6   7   8   9   10
11. _____ Giving and receiving criticism
       1   2   3   4   5   6   7   8   9   10

12. _____ Making good decisions
1 2 3 4 5 6 7 8 9 10

13. _____ A thankful spirit
1 2 3 4 5 6 7 8 9 10

14. _____ Allowances and financial
responsibility
1 2 3 4 5 6 7 8 9 10

15. _____ Coping with guilt
1 2 3 4 5 6 7 8 9 10

16. _____ A positive view of authority
1 2 3 4 5 6 7 8 9 10

17. _____ Learning to follow through
1 2 3 4 5 6 7 8 9 10

Child's name _____

Current age _____

Date of this record update _____

✓ = Current Area of Focus
/ = Successful Performance

(Circle Current Status)

Poor   Great
1   2   3   4   5   6   7   8   9   10

1. _____ Self-esteem
        1   2   3   4   5   6   7   8   9   10
2. _____ The art of friendship
        1   2   3   4   5   6   7   8   9   10
3. _____ Commitment to family
        1   2   3   4   5   6   7   8   9   10
4. _____ Learning about sex
        1   2   3   4   5   6   7   8   9   10
5. _____ Family traditions
        1   2   3   4   5   6   7   8   9   10
6. _____ A heart for God
        1   2   3   4   5   6   7   8   9   10
7. _____ Chores and responsibility
        1   2   3   4   5   6   7   8   9   10
8. _____ Dealing with death
        1   2   3   4   5   6   7   8   9   10
9. _____ Honesty
        1   2   3   4   5   6   7   8   9   10
10. _____ Handling stress
        1   2   3   4   5   6   7   8   9   10
11. _____ Giving and receiving criticism
        1   2   3   4   5   6   7   8   9   10

12. _____ Making good decisions
       1 2 3 4 5 6 7 8 9 10
13. _____ A thankful spirit
       1 2 3 4 5 6 7 8 9 10
14. _____ Allowances and financial
            responsibility
       1 2 3 4 5 6 7 8 9 10
15. _____ Coping with guilt
       1 2 3 4 5 6 7 8 9 10
16. _____ A positive view of authority
       1 2 3 4 5 6 7 8 9 10
17. _____ Learning to follow through
       1 2 3 4 5 6 7 8 9 10

About the Author

PAUL LEWIS is the creator and editor of *Dads Only* newsletter and *Dad Talk* tapes, which his Family Development Foundation publishes for thousands of subscribers across America. He is a talented graphic designer, coauthor of *Givers, Takers, and Others Kinds of Lovers* with Josh McDowell, and author of *Famous Fathers,* a book and video series. He and his wife, Leslie, have five children and live in California.

DADS ONLY editor, Paul Lewis invites you to join the busy fathers who read...

DADS ONLY Newsletter

As a subscriber you receive:

Six, bi-monthly newsletters jammed with quick-reading tips, research and the creative ideas you need to "win" with your wife and children. PLUS...

Two, semi-annual "DAD TALK" cassettes featuring, in-depth interviews with leading experts on parenting, marriage and family life issues.

Clip and mail to: **DADS ONLY, P.O. Box 340, Julian, CA 92036**

POCKET GUIDES
NEW FROM TYNDALE

■ *Family Budgets That Work* by Larry Burkett. Customize a budget for your household with the help of this hands-on workbook. By the host of the radio talk show "How to Manage Your Money." 72-0829-6 $2.25.

■ *Landing a Great Job* by Rodney S. Laughlin. Here are the essentials of a successful job hunt. Everything you need—from finding openings to closing interviews, and accepting offers. 72-2858-0 $2.25.

■ *Surefire Ways to Beat Stress* by Don Osgood. A thought-provoking plan to help rid your life of unhealthy stress. Now you can tackle stress at its source—and win. 72-6693-8 $2.25.